BOOKS BY ERIC PANKEY

APOCRYPHA

APOCRYPHA

POEMS BY

ERIC PANKEY

New York

ALFRED A. KNOPF

1991

Acknowledgment is made to the editors of the following journals in which versions of the following poems were originally published:

ANTAEUS: *Icon, In the Mode of Confession, The Map, Triptych*

THE BLACK WARRIOR REVIEW: *Serenade*

BOSTON LITERARY REVIEW: *Allegory of Doubt, Diptych*

CINCINNATI POETRY REVIEW: *Fool's Gold*

DELMAR: *Exegesis, The Reason*

DENVER QUARTERLY: *The Holly and the Ivy, The Plum on the Sill, Provision*

THE GETTYSBURG REVIEW: *The History of the World, Milk Glass, Te Deum Laudamus*

GULF COAST: *At Dummerston Bridge*

THE IOWA REVIEW: *In Memory, Tenebrae*

THE JOURNAL: *Anniversary Ode, Expulsion from the Garden, Nocturne*

THE KENYON REVIEW: *Deposition, Eschatology, Formal Concerns*

THE NEW CRITERION: *After the Burial*

THE NEW YORKER: *Abstraction, Nightshade, When the Wood is Green*

POETRY: *Clarity, For Luck, Memory of Heaven*

PRAIRIE SCHOONER: *The Angel's Departure, Palm Sunday, The Weekend Gardener*

THE QUARTERLY: *Apocrypha, Midsummer Vestments*

RIVER STYX: *The Clairvoyant, Eclogue, Neighbor, Sortilege*

SPORT: *The Continuance, The Rumor of Hope*

Generous grants from the Ingram Merrill Foundation and The National Endowment for the Arts allowed me the time and space to complete this collection. Sincere thanks to Jennifer Atkinson and Jan Weissmiller for their advice and attention.

Library of Congress Cataloging-in-Publication Data

Pankey, Eric, 1959–
    Apocrypha : poems / by Eric Pankey. — 1st ed.
      p.   cm.
    ISBN 0–679–40617–4
    I. Title.
PS3566.A575A87   1991   91–52719
811'.54—dc20   CIP

Manufactured in the United States of America
First Edition

To DAVID and JO ELLEN,
in memory of our mother and father

What good is it that the earth is justified,
That it is complete, that it is an end,
That in itself it is enough?

WALLACE STEVENS

May the gentle mountains and the bells of the flocks
Remind us of everything we have lost,
For we have seen on our way and fallen in love
With the world that will pass in a twinkling.

CZESLAW MILOSZ

CONTENTS

IV   *ARGUMENTS*

V   *DEPARTURES*

VI   *RECONSTRUCTIONS*

APOCRYPHA

PRAYER

What then but to give in,
Having felt the rush of the fugitive
Released as easily as a breath,
Having been burnished like beach glass,
Crushed and left whole,
Between spirit, between spear point
And forge? What then but rage
That when spent rages
As dogged surrender? Sweet,
Sweet anchor, how long
Your hook held.

I NOCTURNES

NOCTURNE

Soon enough night will have its dominion.
For now surfaces abide. The pink
Blooms and shadows on the tidal flood
And the full sanctuary of the salt marsh
Beneath this sky persist and thus rescind
The worn urgency of the early moon.

He walks awhile, and senses still
The rank wreckage of the low tide.
Smeared reflections double the moored hulls.
Asparagus, head-high and feathery,
Otherworldly in its bluish lace,
Sways against the stiffness of marsh grass.

He walks awhile among these shades.
Dusk is this round water, this uneven ground.

NIGHTSHADE

Those shadows, those flame-shapes below,
Are a grove, trees that in darkness
Give off a damp scent—clove dust,
But sweeter. As he tries to explain
He feels defeated, because he knows what he senses
Is changing, momentary, brought on the wind.
Surely she notices it too. Not berry,
But the leatheriness of bark, the skin of berries.
The seed. Rain after a season of rain.
She notices the long distance they have come.
It is as if the evening began in the valley
Below them, and now makes its way up the incline.
Nightshade, she says. One word.
And everything he has said seems paraphrase.
The air, sweet and bitter, is gone,
Lost to chill, to shade giving way
To the general dark. It is her hand
In his he thinks of now.
Her hands. Not their tenderness,
But how one year they wove
The viny bittersweet into wreaths,
Which she gave away as gifts.
When they finished their work, he brought her hands,
Cut and scraped, to his mouth and kissed them.
He put her cupped hands over his face
And breathed deep the air held within them.

AT DUMMERSTON BRIDGE

It's not the bridge crossing the river,

But what is half-seen beyond it

—Viridescence, what she knows is forest,
The air gin and pitch, the shade
Of the understory and ledged bank—

That divines the night to come.

The stars are scrimshaw and the dusk
Warm with a hurry of blurred lights.

The whippoorwill echoes its name,

A compensatory music for one
Who is drawn to it, for one called back.

ANNIVERSARY ODE

At first the air sustained us. It was not spice,
Not cardamom, not orange, not resin and frost.

Around us the braided air was brine and marsh.
We forgot how the hushed moon withered away.

The moon bluing. The moon a barb, a sharp hook
For mending the night to day. What a courtship

We witnessed between the high tide and that gone moon.
What noise. The inarticulate receding

Of water. The inconstancy at land's edge.
We lived and live in that chaos and welcome it.

PROVISION

Between a laugh and rare luck
A man makes provision for clarity.
He is the beholder who holds little:
The moon, what is left of it, reflected light
Drawn as the expression of full knowledge,
Another day's spent endowment.
As in the cold world, the sheltered world,

The air of earth and foundation,
The example overshadows the argument
And is illumination: a cast, a casting.
Clarity is not precision, the particular
Intersection, the crude X.
It is what the tools cannot measure:
The gap, the lack, the verge of arrival.

SORTILEGE

Contact and intersection, a communion
    With the unrisen moon
Troubles the sharp doubt that delves and disciplines
    His labor and purpose.

How level and cutting the flight of swallows,
    Their brusque discord at dusk
And flood tide, when the momentary fixity
    Of fullness ends the day.

Prophecy takes the shape of interruption,
    Irritability,
The witheld. He opens a book at random
    And consults randomness.

FORMAL CONCERNS

The half-known and faceted fragments cohere:
The room's tangent planes, a retreat of green,

A lamp against the shade's disarray,
Plum tree and marsh. The window charts

Reflections, recesses, and speculation,
A layering of layers. A lens creating

Distortion, a bending and realignment.
He sees himself in the glass

Outside the history of charity,
Part of a shallow depth, a wash, a poverty,

Part of what it holds and, in holding, changes.

VESPERS

As night declines into margins and outlines,
Dimensions flatten onto a scarcity of gray.

No scale or plumb line remains to distinguish
The wilderness and congregation he avoids.

He walks always between with the hope
Of extinguishing both the noise and uncertainty.

He prays that surfaces will not give way.
The familiar transfigured into shrouded shapes,

Pitched and whipped by wind, is for him the sublime,
The sublime of the familiar transfigured.

THE CONTINUANCE

Now that the day is adjourned, he returns
To routine devotion, to a knotted rosary
That is nothing more than a calendar,
The cadence and creep of a kingdom come

It is hard to know from the evidence
If a judgment can ever be made,
If he is the one to hand down a verdict,
Or the one who stands, when asked, to hear his fate.

The herb garden, green through the warm winter,
Has been scoured by an abrupt ice storm.
The mint has gone from flower to char,
Yet by his effort (the old sheets thrown over

The garden bed each dusk) the leafless sticks
Stand in their rectitude, and the patterns—
The braids, the knots, the compass—although torn
And skeletal, suggest their once-full form.

Long ago he cut back the roses.
The earth, mounded out of necessity
Around each, is too easily compared.
A pile of dirt remains a pile of dirt.

II ILLUMINATIONS

ADAGIO AND FUGUE

Their acts beyond action—her stalemate, his stall—
Drag on through this drama. Outside—*look outside*—
The goldfinch feeds on thorns, and the day moon,
Pale waxy chameleon, lives on air
As blue as the pewter beneath the flesh,
A cold at the wrist, a fine-veined marble.
Side by side, they look up, beyond persuasion,
A knot of want embodied as other
Between them, a third who lies down with each
When each lies down with the other, who drones
A recitative that advances their plot,
A problem play staged as comedy.
No. Nothing is acquired or acquiesced.
No *yes*. No *no*. No desire to desire
The cause that caused the once desired effect.

TRIPTYCH

1.

His crime, an unwitnessed act, is not eclipsed
By grace. The clinker of forgiveness still burns
But purges nothing. It is his heart, heartless
And heavy, fused and hard, act and aftermath,
That repeats itself: *remember, remember.*
Who would not save himself if he had the chance?
The chance to forget. To let the hammer fall
And the sparks arc brightly outward and darken.
The hammer ringing its true, consuming note.
Who would not sleep forever to such music?
Once sentenced, pain is mere embellishment,
The keenest enactment of extremity.
And then in the midst to be given a chance?
What is there left to be said and believed in?
Who would not save himself if he had the chance?

2.

He is an arsonist who sets a fire,
Who stands with the greatest patience guarding it,
Who risks watching it blaze. Why live as he has,
—Denying an irrevocable verdict,
Having once believed in its baroque logic,
So convoluted that it turned like a fugue,
Turned and turned until its lullaby lulled
Him, until the heavens seemed fullness, their blue
Of a fresco, faded and fractured, housing
A host of angels and the hidden ransom?
Now, deeply in debt, indentured, what he knows
Of faith is the anaphora of questions,
The meager profit of hedging. The two thieves

On either side of Christ knew the body's weight,
But one forsook its momentum, its slow descent.

3.
Today in paradise a level table
Is the measure of levelness. The acorn
Litter and pine needles in the shade of pine
And oak are all of green and gold that still glows.
A bell hung in the low crabapple *tings*, *tings*
Above the knot and buckle of roots. The ground,
Undercut by moles, gives way beneath his feet,
The weight of his untransfigured form. That's all
He knows of flight: the plowed-up ground giving way.
Here the table is his measure, what he holds
As true. Upon it nothing tips, tilts, or falls.
There are tremors, and the plaster's hairline cracks,
Unlike the ephemeral lightning, branch down
The walls and stay. No matter the magnitude
Nothing upon the table tips, tilts, or falls.

APOCRYPHA

One argued that the manuscript
Could not be authentic. It lacked spirit.

One stressed that the word they'd translated
As *earth* should be, in fact, *clay*.

Another agreed that such attention
Was important, but at this time deviated
From the intent of their inquest.

Soon they forgot the fragmented scripture
As each interrupted the other.

The one standing column, which stood
At the edge of what they believed
To be the edge of the city,

Counted the hours. Its shadow
Lengthened and shortened and lengthened.

NEIGHBOR

Although good seed was sown in the field,
A neighbor came at night and sowed weeds.
Still, among the rugged stalks of thistle,
Among the stinging nettle, corn grew.
At harvest time, weeds were gathered first.
Reapers bound the still-green waste in bundles
With rope, and in a wet fallow field
Burned each bundle separately. Black smoke
Filled the sky for days. When the harvest
Was complete and the granary full,
Alive with the faint scratching of mice,
The smoke lingered in the windless air.

The neighbor shook out his sheets morning
And night, but the oily ash clung hard.
It settled on his plates, his table,
The whitewashed walls of his house. When he
Stood at his doorway gritting his teeth,
He could taste the bitter abrasive
On his tongue, feel it burning in his eyes.
He stole corn from the granary, made
A strong whiskey to warm his winter.
It tasted of ash, as did the snow,
Which he melted for water and drank
When he woke at night with a terrible thirst.

THE MAP

                        The horseshoe lake
Has been reclaimed by the river. Woods,
Represented by a flawless wash
Of green, were cut, burned, taken
By insects or disease—he could not
Remember and perhaps each was true.

His duty was to draw the map, to pay
Attention to the landscape's details
—Each strategic cliff and pass—to mark
Disputed borders with a broken line.
Still, by the time he finished his work,
By the time messengers and armies

Followed the unpaved road, which followed
The long blue stroke of river, the map
Was obsolete. Few returned and those
Who did could tell him little that helped.
If they talked, they talked of casualties.
No one had reached the edge of the map.

There, for all he knew, the green, vine-like
Branches rising out of a tree stump
Tangled a knot around an axe.
A warm wind moving along the tips
Of the cypresses shuddered like fire
Down the rocky hills to the ocean,

If at the end of land there is ocean.

EXEGESIS

One story gives way
To another, deliquesces,
Until all listeners find themselves
Lost, or following

The rocky path
Over the incline, headlong,
Like two thousand swine
Bearing, not the world's,

But the sins of a single man.
That forking, that branching
Away from a center
Multiplies the possibilities,

But to no good end
Except the end.
Invariably, delirium guides the plow:
The crazy wake

Occasionally straight,
But only by chance,
Pure as pure luck
And as welcome as that.

Between two points
Is distance enough to err,
To take a wrong turn
Or miss a step,

To set the ledge to crumbling,
The matted root ends,
The shards falling
The long way down the ravine,

The deep, fruitful valley
Cut out by the river,
The river that winds
Through each town

Because towns
Grow up next to rivers.
That is the truth
Of history.

SERENADE

All is a tally of remnants and patches:
The wave's pitch and rest, the slopes of greens
That slip into half-tones, beyond salvage

Into quarter-tones, until the variegated
Veers obliquely into smears, the disheveled
Stripped now of excess and particulars.

There is no more fulfillment, no more orchard
Brocaded with camphor and spikenard,
Spikenard and saffron, saffron and

Cinnamon. There are these bodies enfolded
By darkness. A bride and bridegroom
Both turned from the other in sleep, safe now,

Unbound and untouched by the space
Between them. The drone of a nocturne
Lowers its veil as if a drama's end

Were imminent, as if to keep separate
The mundane from the mundane.

ICON

Where the blue paint has cracked and chipped
Away from the Madonna's skirt,

Wood, worn by hands that have lifted
The figure through the streets each year,

Shows. A palm's worth of exposed wood,
Rubbed smooth by the salts and oils

Of touch, burns warm in the stammer
And stammering of candlelight.

She looks down as if not to see
What large presence looms above her.

And if she could see she would see,
As revealed through a tear, her flesh,

A slight curve where her hip would be,
Where even the hand of a god

Might rest after he covered her
With touch, where the men, who could not

Help think that it was immodest,
Took hold and hoisted her above them.

ECLOGUE

Did it seem as if one long day had passed,
That all you needed was for the day
To labor through its hours?

No, I remember each year, how each season
Was set down like sediment upon the last.
I counted the layers.

Did the crooked line of trees bend toward darkness?
Did the light that had wrapped them unfold into shadow?

It is true the trees loved light and the darkness came on.
Love did not bring the light that followed.

Were you content to stand at the gate
And only look in?

I stood at the gate.
It was my duty to stand at the gate.

Did you believe your faith would save you?

I was a doubter like others,
Trusting doubt as a treasure.

Did you trust it the way one trusts that the rain
Will finally stop and it does?
Did you think the rain, the trees, and the gate
Opening into the orchard were gifts?

Yes.

How did you find solace in the world?

I thought the rain, the trees, and the gate
Opening into an orchard were gifts.

III DEPOSITIONS

PALM SUNDAY

Three weeks ago forsythia rattled its sticks.
Now, though not an answer, not a reprieve,
The redbud flowers from its hard black trunk
And the magnolia rocks in the wind,

An ark that carries only whiteness and blush.
The dogwood's limbs have not revealed their bracts'
Stigmata, and for that she is thankful.
Why does He descend into the city,

She wonders each year, into History,
His advance raising up dust, a figure
Of dust, which is each of us following
Him? Dust the wind easily disperses?

And why do we repeat the meager fanfare,
The palm leaves bidding welcome and farewell?
She descends the church stairs and does what she must.
She hurries home to the life that's hers.

Each year she looks out for an answer and finds
Only spring's unmiraculous onslaught.

WHEN THE WOOD IS GREEN

The ample day hesitates, and that brief delay,
That tear in the momentum, that pause,
Is, for one moment, consolation.

But for whom? At this station, at this stop,
It is easy to see the crude shambles
A sequence of events can lead to.

Consider the ox pulling a cart full
Of spectators. It does not hear their jeers.
It does not decipher each rut that rocks the cart.

It knows the unbending shape of the yoke,
The shape it works against toward some end.

DIPTYCH

I had looked through these two windows so long
That what shade blocked and what light whelmed
Glared, then grayed, declined durably, darkly,
Until the frame of a diptych remained.
Only a frame to divide suffering
From suffering, the uncertain from grace.
Where but in the worn world is there equity?
In van der Weyden, the Virgin and saint,

Slumped, yet delicate and kempt, seem less earthbound
Than the dead Christ, un-descended, un-risen.
For the mourned and mourners, torture is figured
As a foregone expense. Who could believe,
I wonder, that we are conceived in love?
The anvil wears away at the sledge.
I can hear it out there—*dink, dink, dink*—a dark
Undappled, undivided by the maker's hand.

TENEBRAE

How can we doubters explain the midday dark
When such an elaborate system of spars
And crossbeams propped it up? Though scaffolded,
Dark fell like heavy canvas, slack, unfolded,
A weight no wind could alter, a torn mainsheet
Tenting the sinking deck. Underfoot
This land is a wreck of wheel ruts and gravel,
Crazed with aftermarks, a hill that levels
Here where the killing's done. His body, unbroken
And lifeless, tackled down under the open
Shadows, seems in their arms a drowned man's,
Except for the wash of blood on his feet and hands.
How can we believe his tomb will stand
Emptied, cenotaph to a god and man?

THE DEPOSITION

Dead weight in their embrace,
An accommodation,

A crude translation into the temporal,
The body becomes its form:

Battered and commonplace,
Flawed enough to be true.

They maneuver it clumsily, without grace,
The center of gravity

A fulcrum for their thoughts
As it's braced and lowered,

Commended to the turned earth before nightfall.
A form requires no faith.

Their doubt is faith in form.

THE RESTORATION OF CALM

A place to rest
 Even if borrowed
Demands a bargain,
 A long passion,
A played-out drama,
 That leaves us here:
At intermission
 When what we had longed for
Was interlude,
 A well-carpentered bridge,
A song,

And after such comfort,
 Resolution.
Resolution's trouble
 Is its faith
In an ending.
 It can make a bed
Out of granite and basalt,
 A paradise of dust.
And whatever is sealed
 Beneath it
Remains.

A weight shouldered
 Is not the world's weight
And sleep, my friends,
 Is not the restoration
Of calm.
 Suppose sleep were sound,
Whole,
 Unharmed, that no waking

Disclosed
    The fragmented,
The particle and the wound,

That the wool-dust
    Suspended around the shearers
(Silver
    Then lost
To the air
    And mud)
Could be reclaimed,
    That recollection
Could mend a broken body,
    That this is what we mean
By *remember*.

THE TOMB IN PALESTINE

Here where no gust conjures the pollen's yellow dust,
Where no accompaniment, no counterpoint, soothes,
Where the hardwood is split clean and the mantis prays,
Whose tomb is this
That these three women, burdened and betrothed,
Seek the dead among the living?
This ground is a narrow marriage bed
From which the bridegroom rose surprised
By desire and the effort a body required,
By the aftermath of too much love.

THE ALLEGORY OF DOUBT

He looks to edges, even to the blur,
The disturbed choppy air of mirage
Because he knows when two surfaces meet

What he witnesses is influence,
Cause and effect. Once, each arch
Of the portico framed a scene:

The brunt and the burial, the crown
And the veil. Once, the driven nail
Divined the lines of incidence

But now, removed, leaves a gap
That separates what he knows
From what he knows, *this* from *that*.

As he turns to leave, he moves his hands
Along a doorframe. Puts one hand through.
Still rehearsing the rudiments of ontology.

THE CONFESSION OF CLEOPAS

The spice and pungent air of the earth,
Rising from where they had sealed it,

From where they had placed a treasure,
Chilled me with its damp impoverishment.

Only hearsay and my slow heart
Kept me company. I doubted

And when I looked there was nothing,
Not even shadows or enigma.

I thought evidence would stack up
Like so many bricks in an archway,

That some final event would wedge
The keystone in and hold.

How could I know the moment I moved
Within except in retrospect?

IV ARGUMENTS

THE PLUM ON THE SILL

The cold at its poles and blush
Of blue at its equator
Do not equal a planet.
Composed as an example,

As *object*, this inspired shadow,
This timorous flourishing,
This dimpled orb, does not move.
Violet and gold, the whole

Spectrum of a grackle's wing,
A static arpeggio,
The plum in its plumness sits.
The linear and mythic

In its presence veer and curve.
Put anywhere it stays put.

MIDSUMMER VESTMENTS

If a line of thought is followed
Long enough it leads to laughter.
There beside the garage, in the gray

Thin shade of noon, is the argument
Of greenness: the fern's uncurling,
A hesitant completion.

The truth is that there comes a time
When the day divides into unequal
Portions—midsummer, for instance,

The sun over the overworked lawns,
The half-moon falling more quickly
Than it rose, pulling down with it

The threadbare breeze.
In the short nights, constellations
Wind through their rhetoric. By August,

What is left of the fern is brittle,
A yellow lacework of remains,
The ruined architecture of a thing,

An arched and worthless fragility.
Given two choices, one is lament.

THE ROSE

Why stand as still as a spindle,
Around which only smoke can twine,
Snagged smoke from a guttered candle?

What does it take? A little heat?
You wait, modest hyberbole,
Like the dome of a Moscow church,

Dusty turban in the dusk light.
The chaste dressed in fanfare and spurs,
Singular, precise as rumor.

Why do you hold in the folds caves
And the arabesque, calendars
And cascades? Open, please open

Up between the infinitive
And infinitude, O my bud,
My rose, my little bishop of love.

THE CLAIRVOYANT

Say that he saw each consequence, each effect,
The pileup of causes that equal trouble
A moment, or some fragment of a moment,

Before the next guy. Say that this is his gift.
That he can feel another's headache, the burl
And cleft of it, can hear the awful squeaking

Of the medicine cabinet door, hear the click
Of the child-proof cap, before the victim says,
Oh or *God* or *Not again.* That the wind outside

Will bring rain, then sleet, and turn at last to snow.
None of the certified meteorologists
On the local stations have come close. *Some rain*

Continuing, but clearing by the weekend.
He fills in words like *calcine*, *declivity*,
And *Babel* in the crossword without a clue.

He is certain that everyone shares his fate:
Living at that unsatisfactory edge,
All too aware that an attempt will be botched,

That joy foreseen is not joy at all.
But others need, he thinks, the pretense of chance,
The badly acted humility and jolt

When the gathered party jumps up and shouts *Surprise.*

THE WEEKEND GARDENER

She stands in the garden and thinks as she does
Of that first garden. The tumbled morning glories
Are shrouded, bound up in a mess of spider webs.
The spider's nowhere to be found. The peonies
Sag a little, their leaves worn red at the edges.

She considers the word *misery*, the word *grief*
And wonders what deep-cut furrow separates them.
She is happy. She knows it. All her friends
Say of her, as if it were the truth, she's at home
In the garden, which she takes to mean the world.

FOR LUCK

for José Del Valle

You know for sure you are lucky.
Luck fills you like the shape of your breath.

Then one day as you are reading it leaves.
It lifts up like the shadow of wings,

With the clean ease of smoke on a cold day.
Your luck is gone. You watch it fly away

Over the tracks, beyond Providence Road
Until it is out of sight. Your luck is gone.

Still somehow you trust tenderness
And all its romance, the fine caress,

The salt on your hands wearing away what they touch.
That is not part of the story.

If I should die, you said in the prayer
You said each night. If I should die before I wake.

You woke and listened again to the bent apple tree,
To the wind work the sweet ache of its load,

To the wren and the air it shivered through.
Luck, like hope, is hollow-boned. Always

There is an updraft to carry what it can.
What it cannot falls upon your head like a blessing.

FOOL'S GOLD

I was not the type to call forth angels,
But if I said there's a swallow rising as it banks
Over the white flat of the rail yards,
Tracing the long ellipse of its hunt,
You could believe me. I talked like that.
I looked to the birds for the perfection of geometry.
I waited for three stars to show up
In the graying sky above my house
To watch the right triangle they formed
Fill in with darkness, with all the true
Unilluminated points of that plane.
The contour of the hillside, the white explosions
Of lichen on a boulder, the worn-away roots:
I disallowed nothing and took solace in that.

Bits of shell, a chipped lacelike fan
Of sea fern, and the porous knuckles of coral
All cleaved, fossilized, to the limestone
Outcrop near my house, a thousand miles
From any ocean. History had gone
A long way without me. Against all warning
I looked straight into the eclipse, looked
Into the light-crowned circle of black
While others watched shadows through pinholes.

The land would rise and level away
From the river, a river silver
As it ran from shadow into sunlight,
A river so full of silt, I thought,
I might walk on it. I'm not talking
About miracles. The bank sloped
So long and gradually that the mud

And slow-moving trunk of water
Were nothing but rills and deltas, intricate
Markings I thought I might decipher.
Each stone in the rift was placed
As if a clue. If the water
Shifted a fistful of pyrite
Glimmering beneath the surface
That too was evidence of a language
I was just beginning to learn.

THE REASON

To clarify and allow
For abundance, for revery.

To be permitted clemency,
A first, if not a second chance,

A taste, a glimpse, the sleight-of-hand
Of miracles and the obvious.

To see sky, gray and pearl, the jay
Blue in the copper beech, milkweed

Seed stalled in the haze, the wooden
Stairs cracked and sagging, and below

A zinc pail tipped over and spilling
A round pool that reflects the sky.

To take what is closest at hand
And set a story in motion.

Not to make something from nothing,
But, as at Cana, to be moved,

Even unwillingly, by need.

ANNIVERSARY REFRAIN

The strata of watermarks
On the pilings—a scumble
Of salts, weeds, and barnacles—
Delineate the increments

Of stasis and motion:
The tip to fullness, the fall
To low, the stall at slack tide.
What is hidden and revealed

Daily surprises us still.
The flood and retreat are not
Measures of balance past change,
But of harmony, wild harmony.

V DEPARTURES

THE GOSPEL OF TRUTH

From this distance, what, she wonders,
Balances the dogwood's level habit,
These crimped-edge petals
That float in the resinous haze
Against a bluff of oak and pine?
They are not candid white,
But a constellation washed
In a splash of watered wine.

Transformed by domestic hocus-pocus,
By her daily observation,
Each smear and detail sings its hosanna.
Greenness and shade and these emblems
Held aloft: the praise
Of all she cannot deny.

MEMORY OF HEAVEN

On earth we loved the waste of orchard, those branches,
Propped up with two-by-fours, tending earthward,
The wealth of windfall having little way to fall.
The rot rotting, the bees barely heard.

How easily romance turns here to logic,
To an attitude almost classical,
To a fondness for ruins, for those well-worn stones
Toppled but still architectual.

Yes, in our father's house there are many rooms,
One for each who makes the long tiring trip.
The vineyards here bear a sour, rugged vintage.
Each of us is given just one sip.

THE RUMOR OF HOPE

1.

Bells. A fanfare of snow. The half-life
Of symmetry. The luster and blush
Of an apple hidden in blue tissue.
A spigot. A fall of ice. Flour and cloves.
The cloven edge of a petal. Rose
But redder. Rose madder. Dissonance.
Marl and peat. A shed full of tools
That will rust this winter: shovels,
Hoes, sharp-tined rakes and leaf rakes.
Marginalia. Forgetfulness. A lack
Of charity. The collapse of the random
Into order. The crab tree's meager bounty.
A suite of rooms. One cello going on and on.
The wind chiseling the drifts. The poor.
What, where you are, will always be with you?

2.

We live in this place of suffering and plenty,
Of music, extravagant noise, a clamor
Of reversals and margins distance distorts.
Here there are lines, intersections, and borders.
Here is light and the obstruction of light.
Here all things are endued with form
And separate from one another.
Here, without pulleys or guy wires,
The hobbled moon inches above the skyline.
An unfordable river teems with fish,
Its water a backwash near the bank.
You left here for *eremos*: a wilderness,
A place without affliction or affection,
Where the absolute is absolute,
Where comfort's shape is formlessness.

3.

To live is to believe the rumor of hope.
I give you the holly's fierce ceremony,
The sound far off of diminished carols,
An angel amid columns and perspective,
(You can already sense the aromatic
Gifts, the splendor, the gold's dormancy.
What will it buy?) the inquietude,
Annunciations and visitations.
See how the branches weave a relieving arch,
How no one looks heavenward?
I give you this pastoral ruin,
This lean-to where animals are fed.
Or is it an abandoned shrine or tomb?
You see these are lean times
And the same set is used for each act of the drama.

AFTER THE BURIAL

The lank leaves offer her a little shade,
But still she hates the dust of the clay road
And noon's bright clang on the cannery roof.
The revivalists have set up a tent.
All day it's glowed with a yellow fever.
For her, the rifted hardpan stands hard proof
Of this world that the body must endure.
The soul, too, like money, she thinks, is finally spent.

THE ANGEL'S DEPARTURE

Amid thunder there's a sound without thunder,
A sound that on clear days she calls clarity.
Days are mostly clear and she hears no thunder.

When she turns she hears a flurry of wings,
Not the blown flute as pigeons stumble to flight,
Not the low shriek and complaint of gulls,

But a wide yoke of wings, a well-balanced scale.
The air is still now against her, but a wind,
Turbulent and sudden, stirs up debris

Out in the marsh. The small storm, as wide as arms
Outstretched, wheeling over the cowlicked grasses
Wheels away from her taking its judgment and relief.

DIALOGUE AS REQUIEM

Not this again. Yes, again. *Not this again.*
No bargains are struck. What now could they alter?
Pain was proclamation, the blurred form of *near*

That pressed like a bone against skin, unordained.
Pain is survived. Given in to, it leaves.
Call that a bargain if you like. That look,

You remember, without threshold acknowledged
Lucidity and forgiveness, saw beneath
And beyond to underpinnings and aftermath.

Pain declared her body. Remember that look?
The one the tortured offers the torturer?
Call it courtesy and surprise. *No, not this.*

MILK GLASS

What was left to her she now leaves to me:
Milk glass, a near-flat bowl with fluted edges,
A trifle that sits on the sideboard

As her sole marker. Its blue translucence
Is translunary, an overcast:
Ice that has no ancestor in ember,

But is a source and receptacle of light,
This morning's light the blue of backlit clouds.
She claimed her inheritance, hiding the bowl

On the day of her mother's funeral
And taking it finally when she moved away.
A child's act of theft that imbued for her

The bowl with pricelessness.
And so her gift is a gift of contraband.
No one is left who could accuse her.

The bowl sits on the sideboard, its cold beauty
As welcome as frost on the window, hard frost
That daybreak will not melt away.

THE HOLLY AND THE IVY

The ivy, a worn-out green next to the gray
Of this morning, shivers its useless rigging
Against the bluster and falter of wind.

Wound round a badly pruned maple, the ivy
Is all the green I can cope with after ice
And snow and ice again. The grass, thatch and straw,

Is barely thatch and straw. A thin, coarse cover
Over the frozen mud. That high branch I lopped off
Left an oozing stump—cross-cut and pale amber—

That oozed until the cold clamped down and sealed it shut.
Austerity is decorum,
The potential lack of any potential.

No need yet to unfold a furrow. The gray
Day is an unturned grindstone, a symmetry
Of bluntness, a disc marked and marred by edges.

It is Christmas time and the Christ child is born.
Yes, I have left the holly unacknowledged,
As if to undercut the evergreen world,

As if to say this is the end, beyond hope.

IN MEMORY

If the world is created from the Word,
What can I hear amid the noise of that one
Assertion and all that rattles and diminishes

In its wake: the mockingbird's trill and grate,
The sluice and overlap where the creek narrows,
The dragonfly needling through the humid air?

And what will I hear when words are no more?
I cannot hear you now, ash-that-you-are,
My beloved, who in your passion and error,

In what was your life gave life to me,
My life from the life of your blunt body
That is no more. If I believe that Christ

Is risen, why can't I believe that we too
Will be risen, rejoined, and relieved
Of the world's tug and the body's ballast?

We are asked to testify, to bear
Witness to what we have seen and heard,
And yet our hope is in the veiled and silenced.

I take comfort in your silence,
In the absence of the voice that voiced your pain.
The body apart from the spirit is dead

But that does not mean the spirit is dead.

VI RECONSTRUCTIONS

THE HISTORY OF THE WORLD

Cumbersome grief, grief,
By its form fragmentary, is now our history.

Before history there was only prologue
And preparation. One moment of regret.

One regretted moment. Where, you ask,
Is the angel, the hovering angel,

Who stayed without soliloquy, without comment,
Whose presence was verdict and not annunciation?

How long will it be between call and response?
You see, I have built a cathedral

To every dodge and contrivance. For each brute act.
The structures are complete and now remains

The hard work of fashioning bells.
The cast and recasting. The lugging and hauling up.

And then? The toll—a three-note scale,
A song that calls us to celebrate and mourn

That each day is not the day of judgment.

TE DEUM LAUDAMUS

Out on the Sound
The mottled dark is alloy:
Umber and amethyst, the thorn's

Blue base and pale hook,
Iron filings and ash: all crushed
And forged. A mock

Goldleaf, crumpled, tarnished,
Pilled with motes of rust,
Foil torn where ridges jut

And clouds break, where houselights
Cast out and the snares
Of branches are sprung

By the wind's slightest nudge.
The workmanship is slapdash.
Behind the serenade

A discordancy
Guts and cleans the night,
A dirge without ruth,

Without apology,
That clangs and clangs,
On how the deed

And the sentence are never just.

IN THE MODE OF CONFESSION

If it is true that evil exists,
And that he knows it by reflection,
That he does not speculate, but knows
The workings of such a dark sweet hive,

Then every structure his hands have built
Is obstacle and every fabric
Stitched together remains disguise.
He manages to hide his crime.

Although in the mode of confession,
He does not ask for forgiveness.
He is unworthy, thus worthy of grace.
He asks for a practical miracle:

To relive the act, to undo the done.

ABSTRACTION

1.
The eyesore on the beach was torn down.
The charred half-rafter hanging over
The gutted, broken frame and rubble
Fell last, fell as it should have fallen,
Undercut by flames, unsupported,
First. In three swipes the crane's shovel drove
The house down and raised cold cinder smoke.
The seagulls, mewling their childlike cries,
Pulled themselves into lumbering flight,
Outward from the pilings and then back,
A haphazard, elliptical chart,
Outward from the pilings and then back.

2.
He wanted to know she wanted him.
He wanted her to want him, to know
She wanted him without his asking,
Without hinting or soliciting.
To be wanted was what he wanted.
The ruined formula of his want
Was that he wanted. How could he know
What influence, what small coercion
His expectation had on her want,
The purity of her missing want?
He believed it to be missing, although
In this somber farce, how could he know?

3.

This will be his home: the foundation,
The stairway, the framed-in walls open
For now on all sides. The rooms seem small,
The halls narrow, too narrow to pass
Through together. When the doors are hung,
Perhaps, when the drywall and clapboards
Are hammered into place, perhaps then
The space will not seem so closed. The plans
Denied limits: luminous white lines
Opened the field of blue they enclosed.
He prefers the abstract design to this:
A place to live, a room for each need.

WITH WHAT TO MEASURE THE WORLD

A hammer's heft.
Perhaps a wedding vow.
The permanence of dye.
The faded hue that's left.

The cast of a lantern.
The shape of a wound.
The curves and abstractions
That attempt to discern

The difference between x
And y. The tide's slack mood.
A ceiling smudged with soot.
The world, no less.

SCAFFOLDING

They spent a long time on the temporary structure,
Until the edifice, framed by cross planks and ladders,
Seemed a graph of idealized details: the corbel's bent
Disfigured figure, the flawed soldering on the stained glass,
The spade-like spear points and stone crosses. The scaffolding's
Grid, wobbly underfoot, stood sturdy enough to last
The disassembly. Each stone marked for the reconstruction.
Each ornament heavy with its function and excess.
A lintel next to a gutter, a statue's domed niche
Sideways beside the cornerstone, seraphim and saints
In the quiet chaos before recongregation,
Set down for the time being in a jumble on tarps.

CLARITY

I hear, between *always* and *to be*,
The music of hinges, the one note
The rust will finally put to rest.
But today it opens.
We live in a splendor diminished
By particulars and yet the blue
Of the bluefish against the knife blade
Reveals its amber and violet.
Secrets grant us an extravagance
Of confidences. A salve. A cure.
A flicker lingers on the suet.
Grackles and chickadees
Circle and dive but it holds tight.
A flicker lingers on the suet.
A peck. A smear of red and it's gone.

EXPULSION FROM THE GARDEN

So they learned to build tools.
All night spent working an edge
Onto a stone the day dulls.
Birth, weather, and leverage

Are their sciences, the work
Of their imagination.
Trial and error (spear, hook,
Net) make up their creation.

How to cut a straight furrow.
How to tie a sling to hold
A child and still work the plow.
What to use now. What to hoard.

Whatever works. A broken
Axe must be mended. The stone
Wedged well into the socket,
Bound tight and, once again, honed.

There is always work to do.
The child to be comforted.
A night of dreams to get through
Before the day has even started.

ESCHATOLOGY

Candor and clamor at the end of things
Glares and rings in a grammar that gives
Each word its place through clairvoyance.

It is not the lure of a past, gray
In summer drizzle at its worst, the morning
Poised at the gate, not exile from that garden

That instills nostalgia and brooding,
But a belief that joy will come,
That joy is relief and not a homecoming.

Although each sign, each cruelty, each promise
Has led to *here*, the tick of the escapement
And steady lunge and pause of the second hand

Go on. The mockingbird's song and the lily,
Fragmented and fragrant, respectively, fill
The last days as they filled the first.

Eric Pankey was educated at the University of
Missouri and the University of Iowa. His first
book of poems, *For the New Year*, received the
Academy of American Poets' Walt Whitman
Award in 1984. His second book, *Heartwood*,
was published in 1988. He has received grants
from the Ingram Merrill Foundation and the
National Endowment for the Arts. He is Direc-
tor of the Writing Program at Washington University in St. Louis.

A NOTE ON THE TYPE

This book is set in Waverley, introduced by the Intertype Corporation in 1941, and named for the hero of Sir Walter Scott's novel. In actuality it is very close to Walbaum, named for Justus Erich Walbaum, a type founder at Goslar and Weimar in the late eighteenth and early nineteenth century, whose type was introduced into England in the 1920's and made available worldwide by the Monotype Corporation. Aside from a certain heaviness of the Waverley (as opposed to the crisp lightness of Walbaum), there are very few details in which they differ.

COMPOSITION BY HERITAGE PRINTERS, INC.,
CHARLOTTE, NORTH CAROLINA

PRINTED AND BOUND BY HALLIDAY LITHOGRAPHERS,
WEST HANOVER, MASSACHUSETTS

DESIGNED BY HARRY FORD